A PLACE *to* DREAM

Lynne Blackman *and* Kathy Corey

PHOTOGRAPHS *by* NANCY PALUBNIAK

WARNER  TREASURES®

PUBLISHED BY WARNER BOOKS

A TIME WARNER COMPANY

Grateful acknowledgment is given for permission to quote from the following: From the book *She Had Some Horses*. Copyright © 1982 by Joy Harjo. Used by permission of the publisher, Thunder's Mouth Press.
From the poem *Four Glimpses of Night*. Copyright © 1935 by Frank Marshall Davis. Used by permission of his daughter, Beth Charlton.

Warner Treasures® name and logo are registered
trademarks of Warner Books, Inc.

1271 Avenue of the Americas, New York, NY 10020

 A Time Warner Company

Printed in Singapore
First Printing: October 1997
10 9 8 7 6 5 4 3 2 1

ISBN: 0-446-91171-2

Book design by Julia Kushnirsky
Photographs by Nancy Palubniak

To the mothers and mentors
who in dreaming their lives
gave us a part of our own dreams.

Alice Hedien Sabin
Marea Erf Campbell
Caroline Walradt Goupillaud
Christy Hill
Ron Fletcher

And to the children who are dreaming the future.

A PLACE *to* DREAM

Sleep is the great mother who feeds our spirits and untangles the threads of our daily lives so that we can wake to weave a new day. A good night's sleep is essential to our physical and emotional wholeness. Sleep heals our bodies; dreams heal our psyches and souls. Deep sleep nourishes our cells and muscles and eases our tensions. It is not time spent in darkness.

Dreamtime is a world of color and story not directed by our consciousness. It is a place where we recharge, replenish, take wing, and learn. We are not bound by our self-imposed interpretation of reality. Our dream beings soar over cities, breathe underwater, travel to far countries, and defy time. In our dream world, we wear many faces and are more than one entity, each of whom we can come to know.

Dreams help us question our reality. They take us beyond our small selves and connect us to our gods.

We spend almost half our lives in the bedroom. Transforming it into a dream chamber can change our waking hours and integrate our inner selves. Our Spiritual Self requires a meditative place to sit in stillness. Our Emotional Self needs space for the psyche to stretch and play. Our Physical Self finds balance and health in sleep. Our Sensuous Self desires romance and beauty. There are simple things we can do to enhance our slumber and satisfy our human needs.

A Place to Dream will help you shape your tomorrows.

The Renaissance Women
Lynne and Kathy

Dreams are …
illustrations from the book your soul is writing about you.

—MARSHA NORMAN

CONTENTS

AUTHORS' NOTE

One of the questions we are asked most often is, Where do I find the materials to make the gifts in this book? When we make something, we like to be able to find everything we need quickly and easily. Anything not available at your local stores can be located in our Source Guide at the back of the book. We find catalogs, 800 numbers, and UPS delivery more convenient than driving around town.

We use fragrance oils to scent many of the products in this book. For a complete guide to aromatherapy, please see the Aromatherapy Reference Charts in our companion book, *Rituals for the Bath*.

ILLUMINATION

We begin life's journey by separating from infinite oneness into the light of earthly consciousness. Darkness is the curtain that opens and closes our lives. We have created gods and invoked prayers to quiet the awe we feel in the face of darkness. It is no small thing to turn out the lights and sleep. Sleep requires trust that the world will continue without our supervision and that we will awaken to the same reality we shut our eyes upon. Our ordinary nightly act of sleep is a leap of faith. We learn through sleep that the spark of the eternal light within us continues to glow. As we gain faith, that spark grows brighter.

We share daylight with one another and learn who we are through human experience. Life gives us the possibility to expand our consciousness. Dreams help us explore our psyches and grow spiritually and psychologically. Dreams illuminate the mystery from before life's inception to beyond its closure. Basking in dreamlight warms our souls.

Gentle light helps us dream. The flame of a candle quivers with beauty and reflects the light of consciousness burning in each of us. Its radiance softens the outlines of a room and melts the hardness of our thoughts. Candlelight is a reassuring way station on the path to dreamland.

Turning off the outside light helps us find our inner illumination.

Sleep!...
the balance that sets the king and the
shepherd, the fool and the wise man even.
—MIGUEL DE CERVANTES

1

CRYSTAL ENERGY CHART

Crystals are earthborn treasures with vibrational energies that heighten our moods and impact our health and well-being.

CRYSTAL	COLOR	HEALING PROPERTIES
AMAZONITE	Tropical Island Blue	Prized in the Middle East for clearing the mind's eye and protection from deception. Wearing it in a ring when shaking hands gives a true reading of the other person's character and intent.
AMETHYST	Spiritual Purple	Calms the mind and soothes the heart. It lures the mind into profound meditation.
BLACK OBSIDIAN	All-Containing Black	Acts as a magnet to absorb negative energy.
CLEAR QUARTZ	Pure White Light	Vibrates with cosmic harmony and brings growth and awareness.
JADE	Soothing Green	Called the Dream Stone. It brings emotional release and makes prophetic dreams happen in real life.
TOPAZ	Sunshine Gold	Grants insights into the soul's connection to the infinite.

CRYSTAL HEALING CANDLES

Hidden in these healing candles are gems that release their powers every time they are lit.

1	½ cup glass ornamental container
½	cup beeswax or paraffin
½	inch crayon
6	drops fragrance oil
1	4–inch metal-core wick
1	jelly bean–sized crystal
2	bamboo skewers
	double boiler or electric hot pot

Bend one end of the wick and place it under the crystal in the bottom of the glass container. Lay the bamboo skewer across the top of the glass and wrap the other end of the wick around it so that it makes a straight line down to the crystal. Melt the wax and the crayon together. Add the fragrance and stir to blend. Pour the wax mixture slowly into the glass container. Poke the wax around the wick with the second bamboo skewer to release any air bubbles. Let the wax harden completely and remove the skewer.

CANDLE CAUTION

- Wax is poured at high temperatures and is *flammable*. Handle with extreme caution.
- Never melt wax over direct heat. Use a double boiler or a temperature-controlled electric hot pot.
- Do not leave melting wax or a lighted candle or lamp unattended.
- Water should not be used to put out a wax fire. Extinguish a flame by smothering it.

- Never pour liquid wax down drains or pipes.
- Keep out of reach of children at all times.
- Avoid placing burning candles in a drafty area or next to anything combustible. Moving air will make the flame jump erratically and cause the candle to drip.

INDIAN ROSE
AROMATHERAPY CANDLE

Attar of rose works on the heart chakra and helps us overcome fear. Legend has it originating in the garden of Shalimar in seventeenth-century India. While boating on a palace pond filled with rose petals, the Kashmiri empress Nur Jahan noticed a greenish oil floating on the surface of the water. This sensuous substance was the oil of roses distilled into the water by the intensity of the sun's heat after the coolness of the mountain night. Pleased by the power and richness of the scent, her husband, the emperor, ordered the manufacture of attar to begin in special wooden tubs. This oil remains one of the most expensively derived in the world. More than seventy thousand blossoms are required to produce a single ounce of rose attar.

1	**2-inch votive candle**
1	**2½ inch–diameter heat-proof, straight-sided container**
⅓	**cup melted beeswax**
12	**drops rose fragrance or essential oil**
½	**cup dried rose petals**
	nonstick cooking spray

Coat the inside of the container with nonstick spray. Place the votive candle in the center of the container. Pack the rose petals around the candle. Stir the rose oil into the melted wax. Pour the wax into the container until it reaches the top of the candle. Let cool completely before removing from the container.

NATURAL ROLLED BEESWAX CANDLES

Sheets of honey-scented beeswax are available in over 30 artistic shades. These are the easiest candles to make. For a pair of 8-inch dripless candles you will need the following:

1	**8-by-16-inch sheet of beeswax**
18	**inches of wick**
	scissors or a sharp knife
	ruler
	hair dryer

Beeswax usually comes in 8-by-16-inch sheets. Place a sheet on a flat, hard surface and, using the ruler and the sharp knife, cut it into two equal sheets. Cut the wick in half. Place the wick at the edge of a sheet and press gently so that it is secure for the first turn. Make sure there is extra wick at the top of the candle for lighting. Beeswax sheets need to be pliable for easy rolling. Use the hair dryer to soften them and prevent them from cracking. Turn the edge over the wick and continue rolling with gentle pressure, keeping the edges straight. The tighter the candle is rolled the longer it will burn. To finish the edge, heat it slightly with the hair dryer and roll the candle several times on the hard surface.

We end and begin our day in bed. The atmosphere of love. comfort. and beauty we create here is the one we breathe all week.

—THE RENAISSANCE WOMEN

To light a candle is to
cast a shadow.
—URSULA LE GUIN

LOVE FANTASY LUMINARIAS

The jeweled patterns of these candlelit luminarias come alive at night. Their translucent glow flatters and seduces as they turn your bedroom into a place for romantic fantasy.

1	**sheet white tissue paper**
½	**sheet each of rose, violet, and light pink tissue paper**
1½	**tablespoons each white glue and water, mixed together**
1	**6½-inch glass vase, about 4 inches in diameter**
1	**small paintbrush**
1	**wine bottle to use as a drying rack**
1	**votive candle**

Tear tissue in different-sized uneven pieces with no straight edges. Beginning at the top edge, brush glue onto the outside of the vase. Place a piece of tissue on the vase and brush it into place. Continue to layer pieces of tissue paper on top of one another, brushing with more glue. Cover the vase with three layers. Use the brush to scrunch the tissue for texture. Work down the vase, leaving two inches at the bottom. Turn the vase upside down over the wine bottle and finish the bottom. For a soft finish, use white tissue for the top layer. Let dry. Place the votive candle inside.

Eagerly
Like a woman hurrying to her lover
Night comes to the room of the world
And lies, yielding and content
Against the cool round face
Of the moon....

—FRANK MARSHALL DAVIS

DREAMLIGHTS

Transform almost any graceful bottle, bulb-forcing vase, or wine bottle into an exquisite floral dream lamp that will cast a flattering, romantic glow over your bedroom. Dreamlights are so dazzling that you will want them on your dinner table and in every room of your home.

1	**16-ounce glass bottle**
1	**2-inch glass bobeche★**
1	**4-inch fiberglass wick**
	An assortment of dried botanicals (roses, statice, caspia, strawflowers, larkspur, baby's breath, grass, wild oats, etc.)
16	**ounces liquid paraffin lamp oil (odorless and smokeless)**
	scissors
	tweezers
	chopsticks or fondue fork

Layer smaller petals and leaves in the bottom of the bottle (1 inch or more, as desired). Add taller, vertical pieces of botanicals with stems (roses, statice, larkspur, etc.). Use the chopstick or fork to arrange the stems and flowers. Cut some longer treelike pieces with branching stems (caspia, baby's breath, oats, etc.) and use them to anchor the other dried flowers. The dried botanicals will float upward when the paraffin is added. The branching stems will catch the floating pieces and hold them in place. Slowly pour the paraffin into the bottle until it is 1 inch from the top. Rearrange and add extra flowers if you like. Add more paraffin to fill to the neck of the bottle. Place the bobeche on the mouth of the bottle. Gently insert the wick into the bobeche, being careful not to disturb the dried flowers. Your lamp is ready to light.

★*A bobeche is a glass, ceramic, or metal ring that fits around the base of a candle to catch the dripping wax. A metal washer from the hardware store can be substituted.*

Fire did, and does, light our lives
and warm our selves and spirits.

—THE RENAISSANCE WOMEN

DREAM SMOKE

Dream smoke is as ephemeral as the world of spirits. We can't hold smoke in our hands; it rides on air, carrying our imaginations with it. We see landscapes, faces, and dilemmas rising from its fragrant coils. Perfumed smoke arouses our memory centers and shapes our moods.

Smudging and censing have been done in all cultures, in all times. From the myrrh and frankincense of Notre Dame Cathedral, to the resinous copal of the Mayan highlands of Guatemala, to the heavy air in the Buddhist temples in Asia and the bayberry candles we burn at Christmas, smoke is a sacred part of our ceremonies and celebrations.

Medieval alchemists tell us that a person carrying lavender will be able to see ghosts. Rosemary brings the dreamer good luck and breaks the sinister hold of magic spells. Herbal smoke sweeps the webs of old dreams from the room. In the Far East the smoke of frankincense and sandalwood is inhaled to expand and strengthen psychic abilities. The aphrodisiac scents of jasmine and rose summon dream lovers to our beds.

The power of ancient smoke permeates our dreams.

Twilight is the crack between the worlds.
—CARLOS CASTANEDA

DREAM WALKER'S WANDS

The aromatic fragrance of lavender is celebrated in The Thousand and One Nights *and still scents the mysterious* hammans, *the tiled bath houses of North Africa. Rosemary sharpens our senses and develops the brain and memory.*

36   **stalks of lavender or 6 stalks of rosemary, at least 14 inches long**

4   **yards each of lavender, deep purple, and rose yarn or string**

Lay plant materials lengthwise on top of one another so that the flower ends are even. Triple the string. Tie it tightly 1 inch from the stem end, leaving a 2-inch tail on one side. Tuck the tail against the stems and begin wrapping the long end of the string toward the top in an open spiral fashion about ¼ inch apart. When you reach the flowering part, reverse and wind back, crisscrossing the string over the stems so that they are completely covered. Tie the strings and braid them together.

CLARITY INCENSE

Frankincense strengthens our connection to the cosmos. Inhaling its smoke centers us and increases our ability to meditate and pray. In Egyptian mythology the lotus was the first living thing to appear on the earth. The opening of her petals revealed the Supreme Being, the God of Ultimate Wisdom.

2   **unscented charcoal incense rounds**

1   **dropperful each of frankincense and lotus oils**

Place one dropperful of frankincense oil on one of the charcoal incense rounds and the other dropperful of lotus oil on the second round. Let dry overnight. Place in an incense burner and light carefully.

APHRODISIAC INCENSE

Jasmine is universally prized for its aphrodisiac qualities and sandalwood has been respected in India for over a thousand years as a sexual restorative. Modern scientific research on the erotic effect of scents rates food fragrances, like vanilla, as the only true aphrodisiacs.

4   **unscented incense sticks**

1   **dropperful each of jasmine, sandalwood, and vanilla fragrance oils**

Place ¼ of the dropperful of each fragrance oil along the length of each incense stick, layering the oils on top of one another to blend. Let dry overnight. Place in an incense holder and light carefully.

AMBIANCE

We need time to dream, time to remember,
and time to reach the infinite. Time to be.

—GLADYS TABER

Every home expresses the personality of the people who dwell in it. The theme of their lives can be felt in the sound, color, and style they choose for their rooms. Scent defines the personal atmosphere of a home as strongly as any other element. Drying lavender stalks, a single gardenia floating in a bowl, yellow curry spice, buttery popcorn, or a chicken roasting in rosemary and orange juice stamp their character on our homes. Babies, teenagers, and pets each have an unmistakable influence. Everybody loves the smell of fresh air, but no one can quite explain what it is. From the no-scent of clean laundry to the fragrance of burning cedar incense, an intricacy of smells forms our home's ambiance.

Aromatherapy is the enduring art of using the essential oils of plants to affect our emotional and physical well-being. Aromas repel and attract. They elicit strong feelings and propel us into action. They are exotic, voluptuous, erotic, and stimulating. You can use aromatherapy to create your own ambiance.

Our bedroom is our most intimate room; we spend more time here than anywhere else. The way it smells needs to please us. This is the place where we dream. Scent is a subtle and protecting embrace. It keeps silent watch over our dreams like a gentle guardian and holds private space for us even in our absence.

EMOTIONAL POTPOURRI

Dried whole botanicals in a basket or dish add a modern decorative element to your bedroom. Red cedar, summer carnation, and wild strawberry are released into the atmosphere as you sleep, bringing the power of nature indoors.

½	**cup cedar chips**
¼	**teaspoon each carnation, cedar, and strawberry fragrance oils**
½	**cup dried bay leaves**
5	**cups total: dried blue hydrangea flowers, moss, pine cones, purple statice, and assorted cones, bark, and pods**

Place cedar chips in a glass or ceramic container. Add the oils, blend thoroughly, cover, and let the mixture sit overnight. Add the remaining ingredients and toss together. Store in a tightly covered container for three weeks before using.

PHYSICAL POTPOURRI

This spicy, invigorating potpourri is the hue of sunlight and happiness. Its earthy scent warms the physical body.

¼	**cup vetiver root**
10	**drops each rose geranium, tangerine, and orange essential oils**
5	**drops each lemon, clove, and allspice essential oils**
¼	**cup total: cinnamon stick, star anise, and whole or cracked cloves, allspice, and nutmeg**
1	**cup dried citrus slices and peel**
5	**cups total: pink, yellow, gold, white, and green dried flowers and leaves (roses, daisies, marigolds, lemon grass, and lemon verbena)**

Place the vetiver root in a glass or ceramic container. Add the oils, blend thoroughly, cover, and let the mixture sit overnight. Add the remaining ingredients and toss together. Store in a tightly covered container for three weeks before using.

SPIRITUAL POTPOURRI

Inhale these scents to prepare your mind for mediation or lucid dreaming.

1	**cup assorted crystals or pebbles**
10	**drops each white musk and myrrh fragrance oils**

Place crystals or pebbles in a clear glass bowl with a lid. Drop the fragrance oils onto them and toss. To retain the scent keep the crystals covered. Open the lid to release the scent into the room. Renew the fragrance as needed.

SENSUAL POTPOURRI

This potpourri is scented with Venus, *one of the world's oldest and most sensual perfumes. The original formula was blended and balanced by ancient aromatherapists with pure essential oils—an expensive but worthwhile indulgence for you and your lover.*

¼	**cup oak moss**
15	**drops sandalwood fragrance oil**
5	**drops each rose and jasmine fragrance oils**
1	**vanilla bean, cut into slivers**
3	**cups total: rose petals, buds, hips, and tiny leaves**

Place the oak moss in a glass container. Add the oils, blend thoroughly, cover, and let the mixture sit overnight. Add the remaining ingredients and toss together. Store in a tightly covered container for three weeks before using.

Our dreams are our real life.
—FEDERICO FELLINI

UNWINDING

Ridding the body of tension and the mind of stress prepares us for peaceful sleep. We spend our lives as if we arrived on this planet in separate boxes without a manual for assembly. Mind, body, breath, and spirit are the components of our being, but how often do we connect them? By day the mind rarely takes the time to be totally present in the body. The body breathes robotically, fueled on insipid puffs of air, while the spirit is largely ignored. Mindless exercise, budget breathing, and harried activity reinforce our inner separation.

For us to be totally alive and complete within ourselves we need to unwind and reconnect our parts. When we focus inward, not outward, we begin to build a balanced self. Breathing is both a tranquilizer and an energizer. Exhaling with care and purpose makes us aware of our core and the nature of our tensions. Connecting the separate parts of our physical architecture lets us experience freedom of movement. Unwinding and becoming fully present frees us to *feel* our bodies and be whole.

*When I dream
I am always ageless.*
—ELIZABETH COATSWORTH

DROWSYTIME STRETCHING

Drowsytime Stretching can be done in your bathtub by candlelight. The water should be a pleasing temperature. Add ¼ teaspoon of juniper essential oil to the water. It is a detoxifier that breaks down cellulite and acts as a diuretic. Juniper's calming cedarlike scent aids insomnia. Slip into the liquid warmth, lean back, and rest your upper back and shoulders against the edge of the tub for solid support. Stretch your body under the surface of the water, making it as long and lean as you possibly can. Feel the water removing the press of gravity and lifting the weight of tension.

Stretch through your toes. Circle your feet slowly around, flexing at your ankle joints, pressing through the water as if it were a solid. Inhale at the beginning of each circle; exhale halfway through each rotation. Repeat eight times, then reverse. Pull your energy up to your knees and circle from your knee joints. Concentrate on each movement, making it complete. Turn or move away from your back support to free your upper body. Repeat this sequence with your hands, elbows, shoulders, and head. Move slowly and unite body and breath.

Support your upper back once again. Bring your attention into your body's core and breathe into your center, pulling the air down deeply into your diaphragm. Begin to sway your hips in a natural rhythm, consciously stretching to the fullest. *Your* rhythm is the only right one. Move your hips in a circular motion, creating wave patterns that ebb and flow. Explore a figure-eight movement that begins with the hips and flows through your entire body. This motion puts you in touch with softness and roundness. It is the exact opposite of walking on land, which has rigid, disciplined direction. When we are totally connected, movement rises from the inside out. We move in a completely organic way. A figure eight described in water is the symbol of infinity. It surges out and comes gently back in a continuous pattern of life without end.

Morning comes whether you set the alarm or not.

—URSULA LE GUIN

HOT GINGER FOOT SOAK

Used for centuries by Asian herbal healers for its curative properties, ginger stimulates circulation and energy flow. This purifying foot soak will thaw even the iciest feet—a necessity for a good night's sleep. The tingle and warmth combat winter chill and linger through the night.

1	**3-inch piece of fresh ginger root**
4	**quarts hot water**
	foot basin

Grate the ginger root into the hot water. Slowly immerse your feet into the basin and relax. Have a towel ready to pat your feet dry gently.

TOUCHING

Life begins with touch. Before we see, speak, or hear, we feel life around us. A kick from the womb announces our presence to the world. Newborn infants crave to be held and pressed to the warm certainty of another human being. Babies who are generously cuddled and embraced are able to express tenderness freely and form loving relationships in adult life. Our need to be touched is always present. From infancy to old age the softness of a cheek brushing ours comforts and nurtures us. We thrive on closeness. Being caressed is vital to how we relate to love.

Touch is our first communication, our first shared experience. More than sight or smell, touch is the grounding sense that connects us to the earth and to others. By reaching out we are released from our own isolation. Physical contact couples us directly to another person's energy. It is solid, but it is also pure emotion and cannot exist apart from feeling. It is active participation in life.

Touch is an invitation to give and receive our most basic humanness. The touch of a hand can join two people for life. In one moment we cross from a physical encounter of time, and space, and separateness, to intimacy and vulnerability. Touch ignites love. Two souls or many souls joined together are richer and fuller than any one alone.

Romance is an attitude.
Rekindle your love through communication, closeness, and intimacy.
—THE RENAISSANCE WOMEN

TANTRIC BODY BALM

Tantra is a Hindu yogic practice that seeks to kindle our shakti, *the powerful and natural life force that lights our physical body and psyche. Tantra sees our spiritual and sexual energy as entwined. When we increase our sexual awareness, we touch our inner goddess and step closer to enlightenment.*

½   **teaspoon each frangipani, nutmeg, and ylang-ylang fragrance oils**

8   **ounces unscented body lotion**

Place the lotion in a glass container. Make a depression in the center and drop the oils into it. Stir until completely blended. Spoon into a plastic squeeze bottle. Smooth onto the body of your choice.

DREAM OIL

Dream Oil is a refreshing and romantic massage oil for those private evenings in your bedroom. It can also be used in a luxurious bath. Add 2 tablespoons to a full tub. The oil will float lightly on the top of the water and will both scent and moisturize your skin.

7½   **ounces sweet almond oil**

1   **teaspoon pure vitamin E oil**

½   **teaspoon tuberose fragrance oil**

¼   **teaspoon each lemongrass and thyme fragrance oil**

Pour sweet almond oil into a plastic squeeze bottle. Add vitamin E and fragrance oils. Cap and shake to blend.

Sleep heals our bodies:
dreams heal our psyches and souls.
—THE RENAISSANCE WOMEN

C Y C L E S

Our nightly slumber has both cycles and stages. From waking, we descend gradually through four levels of sleep. In the first, our pulse becomes even and our muscles relax. As we go deeper, our breathing and heart rate slow. In the third and fourth stages our blood pressure lowers and our body temperature falls. This is the restorative sleep we call "a good night's rest." We are completely submerged and the farthest from waking. Sleepwalking and sleep talking occur in this eerie depth.

From this dark place, the cycle reverses and we gradually re-ascend toward the surface into dreaming waters. We do most of our dreaming in alpha state, which is characterized by rapid eye movement or REM.

The first alpha dream state lasts about ten minutes. These states lengthen progressively through the night. The final one may be forty-five minutes long and contains the dreams we usually remember when we wake. A full cycle takes around ninety minutes, and for a healthy night's sleep, we need four complete cycles.

Science has found a correlation between these sleep cycles, our dreams, and our mood before going to bed. The energy that we bring with us into our bedrooms at the end of the day aids or hampers our rest. Meditations and energy objects help us flow into the natural patterns of the night.

THE RUNES OF DESTINY

Seven is a full cycle of time in number symbolism. Three represents wholeness or fulfillment. In Jungian psychology, three becomes complete when you add something from your unconscious self. At night, while we sleep, the unconscious claims center stage.

There are twenty-one stones in the Runes of Destiny: three multiples of seven. They act as our bridge to the unconscious. Collect twenty-one beach, roadside, or florists' stones. Draw these dream symbols on them with markers or paint pens. Toss the Runes of Destiny, close your eyes, and select three. Reflect on the images and let them play their role in your dream script.

HEART = love, health	BIRD = elation, freedom	AIRPLANE = travel, transition
WATER = the collective unconscious	ANGEL = the presence of God within	DOLLAR SIGN = prosperity, money
HOUSE = your body, family	ANIMAL = spirit guide, instincts	YIN/YANG = balance, male/female
DOLPHIN = harmony	BUTTERFLY = transformation	FLOWER = romance
MOON = sexual energy	SUN = wisdom	STAR = good luck
LIPS = lover's kiss	UFO = newness, hope	SPIDER = escape the old
HAT = change	TEAR = sadness	RING = wedding

God...speaks chiefly through dreams and visions.

—CARL JUNG

DREAM CATCHERS

To many Native American tribespeople, dreams hold great power. The Native Americans bend hoops of twigs and weave them with sinew to hang above their beds and babies' cradleboards to snare bad dreams. Legend says that bad dreams will be trapped in the webbing and destroyed by the first rays of the morning sun. Good dreams will float through and enter the heart of the dreamer.

1	**6-inch metal hoop**
3	**yards leather lace, ⅛ inch wide**
3–4	**yards metallic or waxed thread or artificial sinew**
	glue gun
	beads, feathers, and fetishes for decoration

Glue one end of the leather lace to the hoop, leaving a 4-inch tail. Wrap the leather lace tightly around the hoop until you reach the starting point. Tie the two ends of the leather lace together. Form a loop by tying the ends again, and trim them evenly.

To begin the inside web, tie one end of the thread or sinew to the hoop. Loop the thread around the hoop at every tenth wrap of the lace. Once you complete the first circle, loop the thread into the center of your first loop. Continue looping, pulling the thread snug, circling toward the center of the hoop. When you have about a 1-inch hole in the center, tie the thread in a knot, and trim the excess. Glue the beads, feathers, and fetishes to your Dream Catcher.

Dreamtime is a world of color and story
not directed by our consciousness.

—THE RENAISSANCE WOMEN

WIND AND WATER

Feng Shui *(fung shway)* means "wind and water." The goal of this 3,000-year-old Chinese art is to achieve harmony with the environment through the placement of objects. All people and homes have an innate energy or *ch'i* that must be allowed to flow freely for best advantage. Furnishings and personal belongings placed in harmony with our home's natural *ch'i* can bring health, luck, and good fortune. Feng Shui principles find the organic symmetry and balance of a room so we can feel the quality of its life force. Using our own natural *ch'i,* or cosmic breath, we can instinctively create a sleeping environment that feels right.

FENG SHUI IN YOUR BEDROOM

- Moving and hanging objects such as wind chimes, mobiles, spirals, and bells stimulate circulation and send out a positive message. Delicate tinkling sounds are a certain cure for negative energy.
- Living things such as masses of fresh green plants energize a room. Loving, furry pets bring peacefulness and give protection.
- Color is a psychic essential. Yellow represents longevity and blue is wealth and knowledge. Marriage corresponds to pink, white, and red. The color black is lucky for your career. Green benefits family and health.
- Water in fountains or fish bowls summons prosperity.

- Solid objects like stones and art pieces provide missing elements and lend grace to an odd-shaped room. They anchor and stabilize.
- Electrical appliances spark the flow of ideas.
- Shiny objects such as lights and crystals move energy through the air.
- Mirrors deflect negativity and give the illusion of space.

STAR DROPS

Star Drops circulate energy and deflect negativity. Experiment with multiple hoops of graduated sizes hanging one inside another. Attach as many threads as you like for a waterfall effect.

1	**4-inch metal macramé hoop**
4	**yards metallic thread**
1	**small roll Mirroflex (tiny adhesive-backed reflective mirrored squares)**
	small scissors

Cut 3 lengths of metallic thread 15 inches long. Knot the 3 threads together at the top end. Tie the bottom end of each thread to the hoop, making sure to keep the length of each thread equal. Trim the excess thread close to the knots. Separate the threads so that they are an equal distance apart around the hoop. Cut 7 threads of varying lengths. Cut an assortment of mirrored pieces. Take the mirrored pieces and sandwich them along the thread at random intervals. Leave 2 inches at the top. Loop this end over the hoop and sandwich it between 2 final mirrored pieces. Vary the mirrored squares in singles, diamonds, twos, fours, etc. Repeat this process with all 7 threads. Hang your Star Drops from a hook to shimmer in the light.

Sleep, sleep, beauty bright,
Dreaming o'er the joys of night.
—WILLIAM BLAKE

Transforming what is around us into beautiful and useful gifts
makes us aware of the world in a whole new way.

—THE RENAISSANCE WOMEN

RENAISSANCE ROSEBUD POMANDERS

Pomander comes from pome d'ambre, *literally an apple or ball of amber. In medieval times a mixture of aromatic substances like the resin amber, clove-studded fruit, or rose petals were tied into a ball and used to scent linen. Our delicate version is quickly assembled around a Styrofoam core to give you professional results. We thought pomanders were lost in time, but they are reappearing in exclusive gift and garden catalogs. Hang a Renaissance Rosebud Pomander to send out a positive message.*

80	**petite dried rosebuds**
1	**Styrofoam ball (1½ inches in diameter)**
2 to 4	**feet of satin ribbon, narrow lace, or gold cord**
½	**dropper of tea rose perfume oil**
1	**pearl-topped corsage pin**

Insert the small stems of the rosebuds firmly into the Styrofoam ball so that the bases of the rosebuds touch. Make a circle of rosebuds around the middle of the ball. Make a second row on the interior of the first row. Cover the top half of the ball, row by row, leaving a space in the center, so that you can hold it firmly while you turn and fill in the other half. Conceal all the Styrofoam on both sides. Drop the perfume oil evenly over the tips of the rosebuds. Be careful not to let the oil drip onto the Styrofoam because it will melt. Loop the ribbon in half and stick the corsage pin through both ends of the ribbon 9 inches from the top of the loop. Press the pin into the ball. To rejuvenate the scent, add more perfume oil every 3 months.

AWAKENING

We are all seekers reaching into ourselves and toward one another. We are awakening to a new consciousness with a desire to experience the magic and wonder of life, break patterns that keep us bound, and open to a higher power. Our journey is unfolding on psychological, emotional, and spiritual levels. We are uncertain voyageurs struggling toward harmony and peace, striving to find a balance between our real inner and real outer selves.

Each personal quest for growth begins in stillness. Our bedroom is the private place where we become aware of our silent selves and enter the cosmic stream that flows to the world of dreams. When we immerse ourselves in the limitless waters of the unconscious we wake into self-discovery.

SPIRIT KEEPERS

Where does our soul go while we sleep?

In cultures from all parts of the world, ancient and present, there is a belief that our soul leaves our body while we sleep. Many people believe that the soul's experiences as it wanders the night are as real as our daytime life. The adventuring spirit may interact with other beings, encounter danger, accomplish difficult deeds, and feel pleasure before it returns. The nature of its nightly activities affects the way we feel in the morning. A night of fighting can make us angry and tired; stress can make us ill.

The traveling spirit needs time to find its way back into the body. This is the origin of the superstition that a sleeper should not be awakened too quickly.

The spirit is equated with breath and images that move with air: a white dove, a butterfly, or a single feather.

A Shaman's Spirit Bowl offers a portal into the night world and gives your spirit a safe place to rest while you sleep. Hold your bowl in your hands and use intention and imagination to trace the spiraling maze inward from the edge of the bowl. The brilliant colors of the descending spiral represent the infinite promise of your dreams. Blow softly on the feather in the center of your Shaman's Spirit Bowl and settle into its safekeeping. No ill spirits will disturb your sleep.

SHAMAN'S SPIRIT BOWLS

Combine circles, diamonds, crosses, dashes, hearts, arrows, triangles, squiggles, chains, and dots to create a continuous spiral. Experiment with several patterns on paper before you begin. Paint a trail as gilded and exciting as the imagery of your dreams.

1	**can black spray paint**
1	**shallow wooden bowl**
5	**brightly colored fine-line acrylic paint pens**
2	**fine-line metallic paint pens**
1	**feather**
	glue

Spray the bowl thoroughly and evenly with the black paint. Let it dry completely. Beginning at the outer edge, draw simple geometric patterns spiraling inward. Change the colors and the designs as you circle into the center of the bowl. Be careful not to smear the paint. It dries very quickly. Glue the feather into the center of the bowl.

MAGIC BOXES

Mystical containers hold your private wishes and your secret dreams. Magic Boxes are an inexpensive way to adorn your bedroom and turn small gifts into keepsakes.

1   **6-by-4-inch oval box with lid, 3 inches high**
Decorative wrapping paper to make:
1   **7-by-5-inch paper oval for the lid**
1   **6½-by-4½-inch paper oval for the box bottom**
1   **1-by-17½-inch paper strip for the lid**
1   **3-by-16½-inch paper strip for the side of the box**
      scissors
      glue

Cut the pieces of paper to the dimensions described. Place the glue along the outer edge of the larger paper oval and glue it to the lid of the box. Crimp the edges of the paper around the lid. Glue the second oval to the bottom of the box in the same manner. Run the glue along the edges of the 1-inch strip. Glue the strip around the side of the lid, being careful to line it up with the top. Trim off any excess. Glue the 3-inch strip around the sides of the box in the same manner, lining up the top edge and pulling the paper smooth.

I am memory alive
                    not just a name
but an intricate part
of this web of motion,
meaning: earth, sky, stars circling
my heart
                centrifugal.

—JOY HARJO

THE STUFF
OF DREAMS

... *such stuff*
As dreams are made on ...
—WILLIAM SHAKESPEARE

Dreaming in Color—There is a proven correlation between the intensity of color in our dreams and the intensity of our emotional life while we are awake. Many studies show that women dream in color more often than men. A black-and-white dreamer usually sees red first, the color of passion and strong feelings.

Dream Work—Everyone dreams whether they remember it or not. Joining a group or working alone to recall and examine our dreams rewards us with greater consciousness.

Dream Paralysis—The neuromotor response of our sleeping brain to the experiences in our dreams is the same as the response of our waking brain to those same experiences. The only thing that stops us from jumping, running, or moving during a dream is that our brain is flooded with natural chemical inhibitors that prevent us from responding. These inhibitors are short-lived; as soon as our dream and our REM sleep cycle ends, they disappear. In dream paralysis the inhibitors malfunction and we wake up temporarily paralyzed. The best way to break this spell is to make a face.

Nightmares—The terrifying images in which our fears and uncertainties confront us.

Prophetic Dreaming and Telepathy—Many strange examples have been recorded of dreams that reveal the future, or of events happening at a great distance. They are a puzzling and fascinating mystery.

Recurrent Dreams—Memorable dreams that repeat, sometimes after many years. When they recur more frequently, it is an indicator that the information they are sending is important and coming closer to being understood in our waking life.

Sleep Talking—We all have many subpersonalities who speak with different voices. Some may speak a foreign language. Unless someone hears us, or we record ourselves, sleep talking is lost.

Sychronicity in Dreams—Parallel dreams experienced by two people that may occur at the same time and seem to have identical or connected content. Sometimes we call them meaningful coincidences.

DAYDREAMING

Daydreams are the ink with which we write our life's story. In our reveries we review the actual events of our day, changing scenery, characters, and the outcome of situations. In daydreams we have the option to rewrite our own script. Keeping a daydream journal is a positive tool for personal growth when we ask ourselves the right questions.

What character am I in my own story?
What role have I written for myself; is it large or small?
Where am I in my script now and where am I going?
How is my character doing?
How do I feel?
Who do I *want* to be in my story?
How would I *like* my story to unfold?
What did my character learn today and how did I grow?
How do I want to rewrite my script for tomorrow?

Evening is a perfect time for journaling. Enter the answers to these questions in your Book of Desires.

Daydreaming is a way of getting acquainted with yourself.

BOOK OF DESIRES

Our intentions can become realities when we focus on what we really want in our lives. Write your intentions and desires in this confidential handbook. Your words will be an active record of your future.

1	9¾-by-7¼-inch loose–leaf notebook
1	8½-by-11-inch sheet of Japanese art paper or decorative wrapping paper
2	8½-by-1-inch strips of Japanese art paper or decorative wrapping paper
2	5–by–8–inch pieces of Japanese art paper or decorative wrapping paper
2	4–by–7–inch pieces of cardboard
	white glue

Place one of the cardboard pieces in the center of each 5-by-8-inch piece of paper. Glue the top and bottom edges of the paper over the cardboard. Tuck the corners in and glue the side edges to the cardboard. Set them aside. Remove the pages from the notebook. Glue the 1-inch strips on both sides of the center metal ring–binder strip, tucking the edges under the binder strip and wrapping the ends over the top and bottom of the notebook. Place the notebook on the 8½-by-11-inch paper. Fold ¼ inch in on the left side and glue. Let dry. Close the notebook, easing the paper around the cover. Lift the left edge up 1 inch and glue the right side. Let dry slightly until it holds in place. Open the notebook and glue the top and bottom edges, tucking the paper under the metal ring strip. Place the cardboard pieces on the inside of the front and back covers and glue. Place a book or heavy object on each piece until it is dry. Close the notebook and weight it in the same way overnight.

NIGHT VISIONS

All dreams bring valuable messages to us. Even our nightmares are wake-up calls that tell us: Listen! Dreams use symbols and metaphors to help us see things we unconsciously understand. We are truly the only ones who know their meaning. We recognize hidden truths in our dreams by an unquestionable feeling of *rightness*. All night visions are unfinished stories that are complex and incomplete because they are still evolving. Each of them contains multiple meanings and levels of significance. Dreams speak a universal language of archetypal symbols that unite us to one another. They reflect all societies and cultures as well as our personal relationship to them. Our night visions provide us with the opportunity to solve our problems and grow creatively.

Dreamwork can heal our *selves* and improve the way we interact with the world and the people in our lives.

—THE RENAISSANCE WOMEN

DREAM JOURNALS

A Dream Journal on our bed stand reminds us to record our dreams before we forget them. Writing them down helps us remember nuance and details that would otherwise slip away. Weeks later we can refer to our journal to note recurring themes and symbols.

2	**9½-by-12-inch pieces of poster board**
2	**8½-by-11-inch pieces of poster board**
4	**12-by-14-inch pieces of decorative paper**
36	**pieces of writing paper**
3	**feet of raffia**
1	**6-inch twig**
	scissors
	glue
	ruler
	hole punch

To make the front cover, draw a line 1½ inches from the end of the 8½-inch side of one of the larger poster boards. Use a ruler and fold the poster board along the line to crease it. You want the front cover to bend upward to the left when completed. Place each piece of poster board on a piece of decorative paper and cover it, folding the corners in and gluing around the sides. Glue the two smaller pieces of decorative paper to the inside of the front and back covers as liners. Punch two holes on the left sides of the covers. Center the writing paper between them, match the holes, and punch the paper to fit. Thread the raffia from the back of the journal to the front and tie with the twig.

I've dreamt in my life dreams that have stayed with me ever after. and changed my ideas: they've gone through and through me. like wine through water. and altered the color of my mind.

—EMILY BRONTË

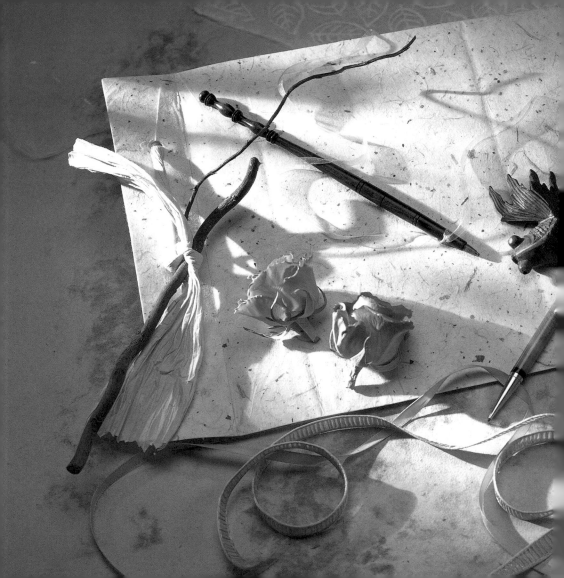

Sleep is a reconciling.
A rest that peace begets.
—Anonymous

LUCID DREAMING

Lucid dreaming is the awareness of knowing that we are in a dream while it is taking place. We can never gain complete control of our dreams, but in a lucid state we can cooperate with their unconscious intent and use them to heal and learn. Vivid, lucid dreams present rich subconscious material to bring to our waking state. They are valuable allies in healing psychic and physical wounds.

TECHNIQUES FOR LUCID DREAMING

- Concentrate on and visualize a specific goal. Imagine how it will look and feel.
- Write your goal in your Dream Journal.
- Repeat your goal to yourself as a chant before you fall asleep.
- Use a memory device like "hands" as a trigger. When you see your hands in a dream notice where you are and continue to dream consciously.
- Be alert for recurring images or frightening figures. The most common incidence of lucid dreaming is in nightmares when we wake to save ourselves.
- Listen for unusual sounds or voices calling.
- Watch for a shift of consciousness like waking up or going to sleep in a dream.
- Flying, floating, or swimming can mark the beginning of lucidity.
- Keep your psychic balance. You don't want to forget that you are dreaming or become so conscious that you wake up.

A wise person once said, "Every demon is an angel in disguise. If you encounter a nightmare image in your dreams, face your terror and ask, 'Who are you and what do you want?'"

Every dream brings a gift.

A dream is the magic mirror that never lies.

—FOLKLORE

GUIDE TO DREAM SYMBOLS

Dreams contain coded information that helps us explore our psyches. Their meaning is often disguised in universal symbols that we can use to interpret them. Not all symbols have the same significance for every person and their message can change from dream to dream. The emotion you feel in response to these images is of great importance.

DREAMING OF:	SYMBOLIZES:
ACCIDENTS	A warning to slow down and pay attention.
ANGELS	Protectors and messengers from the gods or higher Self. To feel the presence of an angel is to know the God within.
ANIMALS	Instincts. If a person represses instinctive emotional responses a hostile animal may appear. Changing animals, especially when they transform into a person, illustrate the desire of part of the unconscious to come to life. A tame animal represents self-control. Frisky animals indicate a change for the better. Helpful or speaking animals may mean that the unconscious wants to help our ego develop. Overcoming dangerous animals denotes growth.

ANIMUS/ANIMA	In Jungian psychology the animus is a women's inner male voice. A man's inner female voice is his anima. The animus represents thought; the anima represents feeling. They usually appear in human form.
ANXIETY	Energy trapped in the unconscious that we do not use and do not integrate appropriately.
BIRDS	Freedom, spirit, and elation. High flights of fantasy.
BIRTH	The waking of the ego or rebirth. In child-birth a woman is an instrument of transformation. The maternal feminine nourishes and cares.
BLOOD	Vitality and life force. A sign of emotional upheaval.
BODY PARTS	Dreaming about a certain part can indicate concern or disease. The spine is sometimes a staircase, our eyes are windows, and our arms are action.
BUTTERFLY	The Soul. A symbol of transformation.
CATASTROPHES	Dreams about natural disasters usually occur during life crises. Earthquake can mean upheaval. Fire may be passion, purification, illumination, or destruction. A flood may signal being overwhelmed.
CATS	Positive model of femininity. The cat is independent, soft, but very true to itself.

CELEBRITIES	Inflation, dis-identifying with your inner being, losing touch with feelings. Positive aspects of your shadow or hidden self.
CHILDREN	Unfulfilled longings. A little boy symbolizes a new undertaking in a woman's dream, a new aspect of her personality coming into being. A little girl is a dreamer's femininity, innocent and growing.
CLOTHING	Your persona. Changing clothes may represent changing your attitude, lifestyle, or the way you face the world.
COLORS	Multicolors in a dream may portray energy. Each one must be interpreted in the context of the dreamer's relationship with it. Red—love, romance, sex or anger, blood or death Black—evil or elegance Blue—the collective unconscious Yellow—promise or cowardice Green—nature and growth Purple—mystery and the other dimensions
DANGER	A warning coming from the unconscious to get our attention about an emotional or physical issue.
DEATH	Dreaming that you have died can be a sign of your own anxiety about death. Dreams of death are usually about a journey. They are a letting-go of the old to embrace the new.

DEVILS AND DEMONS	Repressed elements of the shadow self. Intelligence or sexuality.
DOGS	Faithful companions, best friends, and fierce protectors. In most religions the dog is a guardian and the guide of the dead to the underworld.
DOLPHINS	All sea creatures bring communication from the unconscious.
DRAGONS	Slaying one is overcoming a monstrous neurotic inner complex.
DROWNING	Being overwhelmed by the waters of the unconscious. Repressed issues or emotions. A sign that the dreamer is dying to the old and entering a new stage of development.
EXAMINATION	Fear of failure. Not being prepared for a test is an expression of anxiety often dreamed by perfectionists.
FALLING	The old wives' tale that if you hit the ground, you will actually die, is not true. Falling dreams mean we are up too high or unreal in some way. Landing from a fall can be colliding with reality.
FISH	Inexhaustible masculine fertility. Associated with willing sacrifice—giving their lives so others can live. An ageless symbol, old even before the early Christians.

FLOWERS	Pleasure in romantic love.
FLYING	Liberation and joy, or rising above something.
FOOD	Taking physical or nonphysical nourishment, enjoyment, indulgence, or displacement of another need.
HEAVENLY BODIES	Moon—the universal symbol of fertility and the feminine. The moon reflects cyclic ebb and flow of feeling and energy. Stars—the mysteries of heaven or good luck Sun—life energy
HOUSES	Sometimes our bodies, usually our beings. The structure and condition of the house are significant. A dream has more than one level, just like a house. Going upstairs may be going into your mind and denotes rational thinking. Going into a basement could mean entering one's hidden past. Unexpected rooms can mean finding inner resources. Bedrooms can denote a quiet place. Bathrooms have to do with cleaning out or purification. Doors are opening to new developments and hallways are passages to the unknown. Windows may be an outlook or an insight.
ILLNESS	Inner conflict, or the need to pay attention to one's health, especially to the area in the body emphasized in the dream.

INTRUDERS	Critical judgments and negative opinions coming out of yourself. Confronting intruders strips them of power. A break-in may signify a broken heart.
KISS	Romantic interest. The feelings revealed, whether you kiss or are being kissed, are telling. Embodies the awakening of your animus/anima.
LANDSCAPES	City—The busy-ness of a city can equate with action, excitement, or chaos in your life. Forest—Stepping into a forest can be an exploration of the unconscious world. It may also represent society. Garden—Lush vegetation represents growth of the psyche and soul. Sparse plantings suggest that the dreamer's spiritual needs are unfed. Mountains—Climbing upward represents attaining one's goals; descending can be letting go of mountainous issues.
LOVER	The dream lover is acceptance of one's inner beauty and self-worth. The demon lover is an animus figure seen as a seductive man with a hypnotic fascination. Having a secret nightly rendezvous can be dangerous to waking relationships.
MANDALAS	Universal symbol of the complete Self or wholeness. A sign to look inward. May be represented as an intricate design, an egg, a circle, a wheel, a perfect flower, or a balanced arrangement of four objects.

MIRRORS	Can reflect one's true character. A cracked or cloudy mirror distorts our view of the world.
MONKEYS AND APES	Our primitive selves in age or development with whom we sometimes need to make contact. They have hands to help us.
NUMBERS	Three means wholeness or fulfillment. Four can represent the four mental functions: thought, feeling, sense, and intuition. Multiples of seven represent a complete cycle of time. Nine may signify that all is not quite perfect.
OWLS	A small bit of wisdom.
PEOPLE	People represent many aspects of our selves. Dreams give us the opportunity to have a dialogue with them. Sometimes the dead come back to guide and advise us. Speaking with them can help us work out our own feelings.
SNAKES	Raw instinctual energy. Snake dreams are *important*. They are associated with divine wisdom, healing, wholeness, poison, and danger.
SPIDERS	May be the spinners of a tricky web that the dreamer has woven or is trapped in.
TIME	Dawn—the emergence of something new Daylight—sunshine, energy, and good luck Darkness—often symbolic of unknown forces in our psyche, the unconscious, fear, evil, or feeling lost

TIME	Morning, day, and evening can be the ages of life. Concern about time may indicate stress.
TRAVEL	Facing obstacles and getting to one's destination —or not—can mean abandoning negative attitudes, sometimes successfully.
UFO'S	Jung regarded flying saucers as a mandala of hope and divine possibility. The idea of extra-terrestrials appearing from the outside may signal the birth of new consciousness being born within humankind.
VAMPIRES	A black fantasy that drains energy out of our lives.
VEHICLES	Airplanes—similar to flying dreams. An airplane can represent rising above, soaring, or escaping from the everyday. Bus—Passengers may represent aspects of the self, collective action, or going along with the crowd. Automobiles—usually mean our body. Poor brakes may indicate lack of self control. Running out of gas can be a lack of energy. Driving is taking charge. If you are not driving or are in the back seat, you may not be in control of your life.
VIOLENCE	Fear of loss of one's own power or control. Unexpressed rage or desire. Violent dreams often take place when there is an upheaval in life.

WATER	The universal symbol of the unconscious and the feminine, fertility, creative potential, new life, and healing.
WEATHER	Dream weather corresponds to the emotional climate of the dreamer. Clouds may mean confusion, storms are conflict, and sunshine is happiness. Snow may be frozen emotion.
WEDDING	A spiritual uniting of two aspects of one's psyche. Getting remarried portrays recommitment.

MAGIC
POTIONS

We open our eyes every day with a list of things to do and an honest intention of crossing them off in order. Our day has a plan of its own, and we end with more additions than subtractions to our list. An antidote for a crowded schedule is to create a space in which we can enjoy guilt-free comfort.

Pampering ourselves can be done anywhere and at any time. Brew a magic potion and spend five long, gratifying minutes with your feet up, sipping it. If you are at home, lie down, lower the lights, and surround yourself with soft pillows. Savor the process of being alive. We readily give time to everyone else, yet judge it selfish and unproductive to devote quiet moments to ourselves.

Small things are luxuries when we acknowledge them. Nurturing ourselves is at the root of nurturing others. We deserve to pamper ourselves.

Some say that gleams of a remoter world
Visit the soul in sleep—
—PERCY BYSSHE SHELLEY

TRANSCENDENTAL TEA

Red hibiscus flowers add zip and zing to this refreshing tea. Brew and serve hot or in a tall glass of ice on a summer's eve.

½	**cup orange pekoe or black pekoe tea**
2	**tablespoons rose hips, cracked into small pieces**
½	**cup dried hibiscus flowers, crumbled into small pieces**
½	**cup lemongrass**
2	**teaspoons dried orange zest**

Place all the ingredients in a food processor or blender and chop lightly. Store in an airtight container. Makes approximately 20 cups of tea.

CATNAP TEA

Mother Nature's own herbal sleep-inducing tea. Empty tea bags, just like the ones you buy at the store, are now available and take minutes for you to fill and heat-seal according to instructions on the package. A boxful makes a perfect gift.

½	**cup chamomile tea**
¼	**cup dried spearmint leaves**
2	**tablespoons dried lemon zest**

Mix ingredients together. Place 1 tablespoon in an easy-seal tea bag. Makes approximately 10 individual tea bags.

ALMOND LATTE

This hot concoction is made with steamed milk at trendy coffee houses. A large mug will put you in the mood to snuggle down into your pillows and dream.

8   ounces milk

1   tablespoon almond syrup

Heat 8 ounces of milk in a microwave oven or saucepan. Pour the milk into a tall glass. Add 1 tablespoon or more of syrup and stir.

To make almond syrup:

These are the jewel-toned syrups that you see lined up in a row on the back bar at Starbucks. It is easy to make your own instead of buying the expensive imports. The baking section of your grocery store has a variety of extracts. Check health food and gourmet stores for more exotic flavors.

1½   cups water

1½   cups sugar

2   tablespoons almond extract

Stir water and sugar together in a saucepan. Bring to a boil, stirring to dissolve the sugar. Lower heat and simmer for five minutes, stirring occasionally. Allow to cool to room temperature. Add the extract. Pour into a 12-ounce bottle and cap tightly. Keeps indefinitely.

61

*The entire universe
is a beautiful thought.*

—EMMANUEL

Spiritual nurturing and nourishment are as important as food and a warm place to sleep.
—THE RENAISSANCE WOMEN

SLEEPYTIME SODA

Yummy berry bubbles dance in a frosted glass and cool your thoughts. Sharing a soda before you slide into slumber sweetens your dreams.

8   ounces sparkling mineral water
1   tablespoon raspberry syrup
**   ice**

Fill a glass with ice. Add the syrup and the mineral water and stir.

To make raspberry syrup:

1½   cups water
1½   cups sugar
2   tablespoons raspberry extract
¼   teaspoon red food coloring

Stir water and sugar together in a saucepan. Bring to a boil, stirring to dissolve the sugar. Lower heat and simmer for five minutes, stirring occasionally. Allow to cool to room temperature. Add the extract and coloring. Pour into a 12-ounce bottle and cap tightly. Keeps indefinitely.

YOGI CHAI

Scientific research shows that tea leaves contain polyphenols—the same good chemicals that are in red wine and dark beer—and catechins that seem to prevent damage to our DNA. Cinnamon boosts our ability to metabolize blood sugar glucose. Variations of Yogi Chai come to us from many countries and many times.

3	cups water
1	cup milk
8	cracked cardamom pods
1	tablespoon peeled, chopped, fresh ginger
1	teaspoon whole black peppercorns
8	strings saffron
1	stick cinnamon
15	whole cloves
1	tablespoon black tea

Combine all the ingredients except the tea in a saucepan and bring to a boil. Reduce the heat and add the tea. Return to the heat and allow the mixture to froth for 3 minutes. Strain through a fine sieve. Sweeten to taste with sugar or honey. Makes 4 cups.

COCOA FOR THE SOUL

Old-fashioned comfort foods satisfy our souls. They stay with us even as trends come and go. Microwave ovens update and simplify favorite recipes so that they are ready in minutes with no messy cleanup. Cocoa for the Soul can be made no-fat, low-fat, or decadently creamy.

1	tablespoon unsweetened cocoa powder
2	tablespoons granulated sugar
1	tablespoon hot water
12	ounces milk
1	teaspoon vanilla

Mix cocoa powder and sugar together. Stir in hot water. Pour milk into 2 heat-proof cups and microwave until hot. Divide cocoa evenly into the hot milk and stir in vanilla.

Optional: Top with shaved chocolate, cinnamon, grated nutmeg, marshmallows, or whipped cream.

ANGELS

A new spirit is sweeping the world today.
awakening us to the necessity to act consciously
and individually to preserve the preciousness of life.
—THE RENAISSANCE WOMEN

Angels link us to God. In all faiths they are celestial messengers and intermediaries representing the power within us to do good. They guide us on our long spiritual journey to discover ourselves, and know love. Angelic energy is a positive teacher reminding us of our own capacity to act with grace. Practicing forgiveness and deepening our faith is easier with an angel by our side.

Angel encounters echo a cry from the earth to God.

You can never have too many pillows.

— MODERN PROVERB

DREAM PILLOWS

Pure, deep, restful sleep replenishes body and soul. Sleep may open mothering arms, clothe us in bliss, or slip elusively beyond our weary grasp. She is a whimsical tyrant who likes her comforts. Luxury linens invite her into our bed. Puffy comforters and soft blankets piled as high as whipped cream keep us snug, and furry bedmates are safe companions for our midnight travels.

Sweet slumber lays her head on pillows to dream. Beautiful dream pillows filled with aromatic herbs will summon desire, stimulate our psychic centers, help us dream in color, or give us peaceful sleep.

A ruffled mind makes a restless pillow.

—CHARLOTTE BRONTË

SOUND SLEEP
DREAM PILLOW

Egyptian pharaohs believed that apple-scented chamomile prevented aging. Dried cat-nip was prized in Rome and brought to the New World by the Pilgrims, who shared it with the natives as a sleep herb. Its use and popularity as a folk medicine spread among Amerind tribes.

1	18½-inch-square cotton scarf or handkerchief
1	12-inch-square piece of cotton batting or pillow filling, 1 inch thick
2	3-by-4-inch muslin drawstring bags
1	cup sleep herbs—select from or mix: chamomile, hops, lemongrass, catnip, or valerian
1	yard of fabric ribbon, or lace, cut in half
3	straight pins
	scissors

Fill the muslin bag with the sleep herbs. Place the batting on the scarf or hand-kerchief and put the herbs in the center of the batting. Fold the bottom edge of the handkerchief over the batting and roll it away from you to the other end. Do not roll tightly; you want your pillow to be soft and puffy. Pin the edge in place. Gather and twist each end of the pillow and tie with the rib-bon. Renew the herbs as needed or add a few drops of essential oil to enhance the fragrance.

WEDDING NIGHT
DREAM PILLOW

Savory was considered a favorite of Greek satyrs because "it stirred lechery," and sweet woodruff, with its scent of new-mown hay, played a role in Pagan spring rites. The Chinese believe anise seed to be an aphrodisiac.

2	**identical 14-by-20-inch white cotton place mats with lace edging**
1	**9-by-20-inch length of batting, 1 inch thick**
2	**4-by-6-inch muslin drawstring bags**
1½	**cups of aphrodisiac herbs—select from or mix: rose petals, savory, sweet woodruff, orange peel or flower, or anise seed**
	white thread and needle
3	**yards white satin ribbon**
	scissors
	straight pins

Lay the two place mats on top of each other with the right sides out. Pin them together on three sides, leaving one end open. Stitch around the three edges, following the pattern of the lace. Remove the pins. Fill the muslin bags with the herbs and place them on the batting. Fold the batting in half to form a 9-by-10-inch rectangle. Stuff into the pillowcase. Add more batting if desired. Pin the open edge, tucking the batting in. Start at the open edge and finish the edges by weaving the white satin ribbon through the lace. Tie the two ends of the ribbon into a bow. Trim the ribbon if needed.

Lovers don't finally meet somewhere.
They're in each other all along.

—RUMI

... it is midnight. and time passes. and I sleep alone.

—SAPPHO

Scent is a subtle and protecting embrace.

—The Renaissance Women

ASTRAL BODY DREAM PILLOW

Sage is a traditional symbol for wisdom and restores and strengthens memory. Rosemary activates the power of the third eye and has been used since medieval times as a guardian against evil dreams. Place this pillow above your head each night.

1	**22-by-15-inch linen guest towel**
1	**9-by-12-inch piece of cotton batting, 1 inch thick**
1	**round plastic belt buckle or sash cinch**
1	**4-by-6-inch muslin bag**
½	**cup astral body herbs—select from or mix:**
	patchouli, rosemary, marjoram, sage, or lemon balm

Fill the muslin bag with the astral body herbs. Place the batting on the hand towel and put the herbal bag on top of it. Lift the four edges of the towel and gather them in the center over the bag of herbs. Put all four edges of the towel through one side of the plastic buckle and pull snugly. Tuck the sides of the towel in and arrange the corners of the towel to form petals over the buckle.

DREAMING-IN-COLOR PILLOW

In the Dark Ages, basil was employed to repel witches. Natives of India rub this good green herb on the body at day's end to shield the dreamer from nightmares. Devout Hindus believe that basil protects the soul both in life and in death. Lavender is a fragrant soporific that promotes the deep sleep required for a full and vivid dream cycle.

1	**25-by-16-inch embroidered guest towel**
1	**16-by-16-inch piece of cotton batting, 1 inch thick**
3	**4-by-6-inch muslin drawstring bags**
1½	**cups of dreamwork herbs—select from or mix:**
	lavender, lemon peel, basil, rose geranium, or
	spearmint
	needle and thread

Fold the unembroidered end of the towel over 8 inches. Stitch both sides together to form a pocket. Fold the batting in half and place it in the pocket. Fill the muslin bags with the herbs. Put them in between the layers of the batting. Fold the embroidered edge over the pocket like an envelope flap. Renew the herbs as needed.

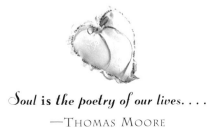

Soul is the poetry of our lives. . . .

—THOMAS MOORE

MIDNIGHT INDULGENCES

Love doesn't bring
You
           Another person.
It brings you your
"Self"

           —A. B. C.

There are two kinds of people in the world—those who get up to greet the sunrise and those who stay up to watch it. Whichever kind you are, staying up late and creating private space in bed at night has a soul-satisfying feeling of indulgence. Midnight space has a sense of naughtiness about it. It is a break in routine, whether it is curling up and reading a fashion magazine when we should be paying the bills, or cuddling romantically with a dream mate.

Midnight indulgences revitalize us.

I was not looking for dreams to interpret life,
but rather for my life to interpret my dreams.
—SUSAN SONTAG

POPCORN AND OLD PAJAMAS

Everyone has a favorite piece of clothing that they don't want to be seen in. It has been washed so many times that it has lost its shape, is wearing thin, and feels like a second skin. It might have been *his* T-shirt or a souvenir, but it is soft and warm and we can't bear to part with it. We wear it to bed when we are alone.

We have an inner personality that doesn't fit our public persona or our own concept of who we are. Hidden among our rational, organized, and efficient faces is an indolent, pleasure-loving imp who likes to stay up past bedtime, refuses to pick up a ringing phone, cries over old movies, and eats popcorn in bed. Honor the imp and let her play.

Indulging all of our needs without guilt keeps us in balance.

> *Love is not a matter of counting the years: it's making the years count.*
>
> —WILLIAM SMITH

REKINDLING ROMANCE

Just as sleep has stages and cycles, so do romance and relationships. First love is based on newness and unfamiliarity. It begins with the surge of excitement at the sound of a name. Our heart quickens and our blood races when we think of our next encounter. Our passion is uncontrollable, delirious, delightful, and we surrender to it.

Time passes, and beautiful actions become routine. In this stage we live without intensity toward one another. We take each other for granted and forget to express our love. As sleepmates, we bring our worries, our uncertainties, and our frustrations to bed.

Romance is an attitude. It is a matter of choice. We can rekindle the flames of our passion from a strong new basis of shared experience and united energies. In this stage we are no longer strangers. We face the world as a team and give fully to our partner every day.

A night of passion can be any night. Take care of all the details. Surprise your partner or plan it together. Check your calendars and set the date. It doesn't have to be an anniversary or a full moon; the best night is *just because.* Plan to stay at home and arrange to have the house to yourselves. Transform your bedroom into a place for romance. Set the mood with scented candles, fresh flowers, mellow music, and inviting sheets and pillows. This is not a night for baggy PJs. Use your loving imagination. Chilled champagne is the most romantic drink we can think of, and it goes wonderfully with cold fruit dipped in chocolate sauce. Keep it light and simple. Don't wear yourself out before your evening begins. A heavy meal or too much activity will make you sleepy. Rekindle your love through communication, closeness, and intimacy. Begin by expressing ten things you value and appreciate about your lover.

This is your night to dream together.

Every day cannot be a holiday, but every day can be a memory.

—THE RENAISSANCE WOMEN

BREAKFAST IN BED
FOR TWO

A night spent together doesn't have to end at dawn. Time spent communicating with one another is too precious to cut short. Plan breakfast in bed for a weekend or holiday morning and completely spoil your sleepmate. Our day-off schedule seems just as hectic as our workweek. But what better way can there be to spend it? A Breakfast in Bed for Two ritual says, "You are special. I appreciate you." Making time for a relaxed morning together is a conscious choice that honors your relationship.

We end and begin our day in the bedroom. The atmosphere of love, comfort, and beauty that we create here is the one we breathe all week.

BRIGHT BEGINNINGS

Presentation sets the mood. Look around for the pretty things in your home and use them to create elegance. You don't need to be a chef. Thoughtfulness counts!

- Brew a pot of wake-up coffee or tea.
- Squeeze or pour fresh juice into wineglasses and top with a mint leaf, or make Peach Mimosas.
- Slice seasonal melon, strawberries, kiwis, oranges, and bananas.
- Bake or buy Sunday Scones, pastry, or bagels. Heat or toast them, and serve with butter, jam, or cream cheese.
- Provide something special: French Eggs, lox, caviar, Canadian bacon, or ham.
- Arrange the food on a bed tray, on a silver platter, or in a wicker basket.
- Place a single garden flower or long-stemmed rose in a vase.
- Use cloth napkins, show-off dishes, and fancy silverware.

It has been said that chocolate is the sexiest of all flavors.

—MAIDA HEATTER

CHOCOLATE-DIPPED FRUIT

So simple, yet so elegant Chocolate-Dipped Fruit is a favorite dessert at gourmet restaurants. We have demystified and uncomplicated this recipe.

10	**each fresh strawberries, tangerine sections, and banana slices**
2	**ounces top-quality dark chocolate, e.g., Lindt, Ghirardelli, Cadbury, or Tobler**

Coarsely chop the chocolate and melt it in the top of a double boiler over low heat. Stir until the chocolate is smooth. Dip the berries to coat them and place them on wax paper to dry. Use a toothpick or fondue fork for the tangerine sections and banana pieces. Refrigerate for up to one day.

PEACH MIMOSAS

Peach nectar is a variation on the traditional mimosa, which is made with champagne and orange juice. Use juicy summer peaches when available.

4	**ounces peach juice, purée, or nectar**
2	**teaspoons peach schnapps**
6	**ounces chilled champagne**
2	**chilled champagne flutes**

Pour ½ of the peach juice and schnapps into each glass. Top with the chilled champagne.

Our lives are a full circle to time's closure. Embrace life,
appreciate its detail, and celebrate the joy of just being alive.

—THE RENAISSANCE WOMEN

SUNDAY SCONES

This recipe comes to us from a man who enjoys bringing Breakfast in Bed for Two to his wife. He likes to vary his recipe with orange zest, almonds, or raisins. Men can make Sunday Scones—and easily! Wow her with your culinary skill.

1¼	**cups all-purpose flour**
1	**tablespoon granulated sugar**
¼	**teaspoon salt**
2	**teaspoons baking powder**
½	**teaspoon baking soda**
8	**tablespoons (1 stick) unsalted butter**
2	**large eggs**
⅓	**cup cream**

For topping:

1	**tablespoon melted butter**
	brown and white sugar

Optional:

2	**tablespoons orange zest**
¼	**cup sliced almonds, raisins, or dried cranberries**

Preheat oven to 425°. Grease baking sheet; set aside. Combine the flour, salt, sugar, baking powder, and baking soda. Cut the butter into pieces and add it to the dry ingredients. Using a pastry cutter or two knives, work mixture until it resembles cornmeal. Mix in the eggs, one at a time, and then add the cream. Add the optional ingredients, if desired. Combine with a few strokes. Handle the dough as little as possible. Place it on a lightly floured board and pat it into a round, about ¾ of an inch thick. Cut it into 8 triangles. Bake for 15 to 20 minutes, or until golden brown. For topping, brush the triangles with the melted butter and sprinkle them with the sugars.

FRENCH EGGS

Scrambled eggs in France are as creamy and soft as custard. The trick is to stir them constantly over low heat just until they are thickened.

4	**large eggs**
	salt and pepper to taste
1	**tablespoon butter**
1	**tablespoon heavy whipping cream**

Beat the eggs in a bowl with the salt and pepper. Melt the butter in a skillet over low heat. Pour the eggs into the skillet and stir until they thicken to the consistency you desire. Remove them from the heat and stir in the cream.

CREATING A PLACE TO DREAM

- Spend as much on a set of linens as you would on a new outfit. They'll be around a lot longer.
- Keep fresh flowers in the bedroom. A single rose will do.
- Install a good reading lamp.
- Send the kids to Grandmother's.
- Consider placing a fountain in your bedroom. The sound of running water is immeasurably soothing.
- Invest in a *good* mattress.
- Prolong darkness with blackout curtains for morning dreaming.
- Change color schemes with the seasons or at whim.

RENAISSANCE

When we began writing as the Renaissance Women, the word renaissance required definition. Now renaissance is alive in everyone's consciousness. It is being used to sell products, name businesses, describe weekend getaways, and make aging attractive. Our world is experiencing a spiritual renaissance, inspiring in us the need to act consciously and individually to *know* the preciousness of life.

As caring human beings, we are searching for personal, family, and societal values that work. This means being in the learning process forever: Life *is* change. We are looking inward and around us to our families, our homes, our neighbors, and friends, and outward to our communities and the planet we share.

We believe that value is found in small things.

People often ask us how we began to write together. We are friends, neighbors, and gift makers whose quests have led us to write and share our experiences. Our books do not come out of research; they come from our living our lives. When we travel the country we meet people who express the same thoughts and feelings. We are listening to this collective voice and sharing what we hear.

Our words are the message of many souls.

SOURCE GUIDE

CRAFT, ART, AND CANDLE SUPPLY STORES
Check your Yellow Pages for stores in your area.

Ben Franklin stores
Michaels stores
Tandy Leather Company

Value Craft stores
Wicks 'N' Sticks

CATALOGS

BEAUTIFUL BEDDING

Chambers
P.O. Box 7841
San Francisco, CA 94120–7841
800-334-9790

Cuddledown of Maine
312 Canco Road
Portland, ME 04103
800-323-6793

CANDLE AND LAMP SUPPLIES

Barker Candle Supplies
15106 Tenth Avenue S.W.
Seattle, WA 98166
800-543-0601

Mid-Con
8909 Lenexa Drive
Overland Park, KS 66214–3837
800-547-1392
Fax 913-492-2742

Also see: Dick Blick Art Materials under "Craft and Art Materials."

CRAFT AND ART MATERIALS

Dick Blick Art Materials
P.O. Box 1267
Galesburg, IL 61402–1267
800-447-8192
Fax 800-621-8293
(carries Mirroflex)

Leather Unlimited
7155 Cty. Hwy. B, P.O. Box L
Belgium, WI 53004-0911
414-994-9464
Fax 414-994-4099

DRIED BOTANICALS, POTPOURRI, TEA MAKING SUPPLIES, FRAGRANCE OILS, AND LOTIONS

Aroma Vera
5901 Rodeo Road
Los Angeles, CA 90016-4312
800-669-9514
Fax 310-280-0395

The Essential Oil Company
P.O. Box 206
Lake Oswego, OR 97034
800-729-5912
Fax 800-825-2985

Lavender Lane
5321 Elkhorn Blvd.
Sacramento, CA 95842
916-334-4400
Fax 916-339-0842

Mountain Rose Herbs
P.O. Box 2000
Redway, CA 95560
800-879-3337
Fax 707-923-7867

Nature's Herb Company
1010 Forty-sixth Street
Emeryville, CA 94608
510-601-0700

Summers Past
15602 Old Highway 80
Flinn Springs, CA 92021
800-390-9969

The Ultimate Herb &
Spice Shoppe111 Azalea, Box 395
Duenweg, MO 64841
417-782-0457

Body Time
1341 Seventh Street
Berkeley, CA 94710
510-524-0360
Fax 510-527-0979

Herb Products Company
P.O. Box 898
North Hollywood, CA 91603-0898
818-984-3141
Fax 818-508-6567

Le Melange
P.O. Box 1166
Clifton Park, NY 12065
Phone/Fax 800 467 0582

Nature's Finest
P.O. Box 10311
Dept. RB
Burke, VA 22009-0311
703-978-3925

Nichols Garden Nursery
1190 S. Pacific
Albany, OR 97321
503-928-9280

Union Street Apothecary
2185A Union St.
San Francisco, CA 94123
415-771-1207

Wild Weeds
P.O. Box 88
Ferndale, CA 95536
800-553-9543
Fax 800-836-9543

INCENSE

Ananda Country Products
14618 Tyler Foote Road, Ste.51
Nevada City, CA 95959
800-537-8766
Fax 916-292-4281

Also see: The Essential Oil Company, Mountain Rose Herbs, and Wild Weeds under "Dried Botanicals, Potpourri, Tea Making Supplies, Fragrance Oils, and Lotions."

WOODEN BOWLS

Weston Bowl Mill
714 Main St.
Weston, VT 05161
800-452-8911
Fax 802-824-4215